IRISH PROVERBS AND SAYINGS

Gems of Irish Wisdom

Padraic O'Farrell

MERCIER PRESS

MERCIER PRESS
Cork
www.mercierpress.ie

Trade enquiries to CMD,
55a Spruce Avenue, Stillorgan Industrial Park,
Blackrock, County Dublin

ISBN: 978 0 85342 846 6

15 14 13 12

A CIP record for this title is available from the British Library

To Niamh

the arts
council
schomhairle
ealaíon

Mercier Press receives financial assistance from the
Arts Council/An Chomhairle Ealaíon

Printed and bound in the EU.

CONTENTS

Foreword   5

Advice, Age, Ambition, Anger,
Animals, Attitudes   7

Beauty, Behaviour, Bitterness,
Blessings, Borrowing, Bravery   16

Character, Charity, Cleverness, Commerce,
Company, Competence, Contentment   21

Death, Drink   28

Education, Enemies, Experience   32

Family, Fate, Fighting, Flattery,
Food, Foolishness, Friendship   36

God, Goodness, Greed   45

Health, Heaven, Hell, Hope,
Humour, Hypocrisy   47

Idleness, Informers, Integrity   53

Justice   56

Love, Luck   57

Man, Marriage, Meanness, Misfortune,
Mistakes, Money   59

Nature, Need   67

Patience, Politics, Pride, Property   68

Roguery   73

Scarcity, Sense, Sorrow, Spending,
Sport, Strength   74

Tact, Talk, Thanks, Theatre, Time   79

Value   83

Weariness, Wisdow, Woman, Work   84

FOREWORD

It was with great enthusiasm that I set about collecting some *Gems of Irish Wisdom* for this book. The subject fascinated me. My book *How The Irish Speak English* had absorbed a number of snatches of dialogue which could have been classified as gems of wisdom but there was a rich harvest still to be gleaned from the Irish countryside, from the lips of great men and from the bright, unspoilt fount of folklore, legend and proverb that still springs whenever Irish people, however long removed from a rural environment, congregate.

I wish to acknowledge the co-operation of the Head of the Department of Folklore in allowing me to avail of the fine facilities of his department and to peruse and quote from manuscripts and published material. To him and his courteous staff I offer my sincere thanks. I also thank Mrs Fionnula Williams, Balmoral Gardens, Belfast for allowing me to study her thesis, *Index of the Proverbs of County Monaghan.* This was of immense help in tracing wise sayings, not alone of Country Monaghan but of many other areas too.

Thanks too to my own family, Laurence Gavin, Geraldine Hyland and Patricia Clinton for their assistance.

ADVICE

It's no use giving good advice unless you have the wisdom to go with it.

Ní hé lá na gaoithe lá na scolb (A windy day is not the day for thatching. (*Scolb* is a rod used in thatching).

Some day you'll follow the crow for what you waste.

Cut your coat according to your cloth.

Neither give cherries to pigs nor advice to a fool.

Good advice often comes from a fool.

Never rub your eye except with your elbow.

Beware of the horse's hoof, the bull's horn and the Saxon's smile.

Give away all you like but keep your bills and your temper.

Don't make a bid till you walk the land.

Never trust a fine day in winter, the life of an old man or the word of an important person unless it's in writing.

Good advice has no price.

If you don't want flour on your happen (clothes) you should keep out of the mill.

The man who won't take advice will have conflict.

Befriend who you wish but make sure you know what side your bread is buttered on.

Raise the wick before darkness falls.

It is foolish to scorn advice but more foolish to take all advice.

Don't throw away the sweepings of the bag until you see did you drop your ring into it.

When everybody else is running, that's the time for you to walk.

If you dig a grave for others you might fall into it yourself.

Give the liberty of talking to the loser.

Stay on the ground and you'll be the best horseman.

Never let your right hand know what your left hand is doing.

A good run is better than a bad stand.

If you do your best, don't mind the rest.

Don't throw away the dirty water until you are sure you have clean water.

Return from the middle of the ford before you drown in the flood.

If you're advised to use a gun make sure there's not another in your back.

If you have to give advice to lovers find out what they want first and advise them to do that.

Woe to the man who does not heed the advice of a good wife.

If you came up in this world make sure you don't go down in the next.

Never put off till tomorrow what you can do today.

Avoid a man with a narrow face and never kiss a man that could himself kiss a puckan between the horns.

AGE

An old briar does nothing but interfere with progress.

A hair on the head is worth two on the brush.

It's not easy to twist the hardened twig.

No matter what our calling, age will call us all.

A man only feels as old as the woman he feels.

To be old and withered is no shame.

The old dog for the hard road and leave the pup on the path.

Sense doesn't come before age.

Strength decreases with age but wisdom grows.

A young woman gets a man's glances, an old woman his heart.

When we are old all our pleasures are behind us but when we are young all our troubles are before us.

If you move old furniture it might fall to bits.

A son's stool in his father's home is steady as a gable. A father's in his son's, bad luck, is shaky and unstable.

The older the fiddle, the sweeter the tune.

Better an old man's darling than a young man's slave.

The old *dúidín*(pipe) gives the sweetest smoke.

There's an old sock to fit every old boot and what's more old boots are likely to be without tongues.

It's no harm having plenty of old men in your life as long as there is not plenty of life in the old men.

AMBITION

Whoever watches for a living man's boots will get sore feet from going barefooted.

On the Irish ladder of success there's always some one on the rung above using your head to steady himself.

Gold shines through the darkest night for the man with ambition.

The ambitious man is seldom at peace.

Possession never satisfies the ambitious man.

There's no stopping the force of a going wheel.

Keep away from the fellow that was reared in his bare feet for they will be hardened from walking on people.

ANGER

A red-hot *gríosach* (ember) is easily re-kindled.

Hotter than a Cluais bog fire,
The uncontrolled Mayo man's ire.

There is anger in an open smile.

The wrath of God has nothing on the wrath of an Irishman outbid for land, a horse or a woman.

Let your anger set with the sun and not rise again with it.

A gentle answer quells anger.

ANIMALS

There are more ways of killing a dog than by choking it with butter.

Don't go to the goat's shed if it's wool you're seeking.

A smithy's ass and a cobbler's wife are often most barefooted.

All their hens are pensioners for, God help them, he married a wan from the city and she'll kill off nothing.

A puckan may be the spittin' image of a goat but he'll not give milk.

It's hard to choose between two blind goats.

Better an ass that carries you than a fine horse that throws you.

A cow is no good if she dribbles her drop.

Cows in Connacht have long horns but the mileys at home milk as well.

There's no point in keeping a dog if you are going to do your own barking.

Wee dogs start the hare but big ones catch it.

A lion is no pet for a wee bairn (child).

The best ass cannot run forever.

No use wearing cloth that the sheep could graze through.

You can lead the horse to the well but you can't make him drink.

A man with no wit has little on a pig.

Autumn comes quicker than a mountain hare.

The last straw broke the horse's back.

The horse that wins doesn't lose the reins.

An engine is like an old sheep-dog. 'Twill work for the man that's used to handling it.

The rabbit gets fat on what the hare misses.

You won't break a wild horse with a silk thread.

The best colt needs the most breaking in.

Many's the shaggy colt turned out a fine horse.

As the old cock crows the young cock learns.

The shorter the *bineen* (rope tethering a beast) the less chance of a broken leg.

The last horse home blames the bit.

May he marry a ghost that will bear him a *banbh* (piglet) and may the Holy Ghost give it the scours for a cruel man is sinful.

The quiet pig eats the cabbage.

No use having a dog and chasing your own sheep.

A cat has leave to look at a king.

A nod is as good as a wink to a blind horse.

Threatened dogs live long.

It's no use praying for fine weather if the ram's back is to the ditch.

ATTITUDES

It's the pebble in the hoof that hurts.

The best way to get an Irishman to refuse to do something is by ordering it.

'Sé *caithfidh tú* an athair do *ní dhéanfaidh mé. (You must* is the father of *I won't).*

The heaviest ear of corn is the one with its head bent lowest.

In for a penny, in for a pound.

The best hurlers are on the ditch and the thicker the ditch the sharper the thorns.

The last place is worthy of the most beloved.

Bigots and begrudgers will never bid the past farewell.

You might as well be hung for a sheep as for a lamb.

An inch is as good as a mile to a blind horse.

The more the storm tries to whip off your happen (clothes) the more you should grip your gallaces (braces).

The man with the broken ankle is most conscious of his legs.

Hating a man doesn't hurt him half as much as ignoring him.

Pressure of business weakens kindness.

Good manners are often better than good looks.

No property — no friends; no rearing — no manners; no health — no hope.

All men praise their native county.

Many a sudden change takes place on an unlikely day.

Everyone feels his own wound first.

A man is shy in another man's street.

It's the heaviest rain that makes the greenest grass.

Initiative is praiseworthy when it succeeds, stupid when it fails.

A cynic is '. . .a man who knows the price of everything and the value of nothing.'

Wilde

Titles distinguish the mediocre, embarrass the superior and are disgraced by the inferior.

Shaw

Bíonn na daoine fasta dáll. (Grown people are blind).

Pearse

Morality is simply the attitude we adopt towards people whom we personally dislike.

Wilde

There is no satisfaction in hanging a man who does not object to it.

Shaw

BEAUTY

Beauty is only skin deep but nobody wants to be drowned.

A pot was never boiled by beauty.

A blind man is no judge of beauty.

If you have no beauty within you, you'll not perceive it.

It's the gem that cannot be owned which is the most beautiful.

The beauty of a chaste woman causes bitter words.

If a mother has no beauty in her face she has it in her heart.

Elegance and beauty are the same thing when there's a man after them.

Always make sure she looks beautiful before breakfast as well as after dinner.

BEHAVIOUR

You won't be stepped on if you're a live wire.

He's a dirty bird who won't keep his own nest clean.

It is easier to fall than to rise.

Burning the candle at both ends will soon leave you without a light.

If you get the name of being an early riser you can sleep till dinner-time.

Familiarity breeds contempt.

If you want to know me, come and live with me.

He has a rag on every bush, more luck to him.

Keep a blind eye when you're in another man's corner.

Man is either a worker, a boaster or a pleasure-seeker.

The Irish forgive their great men when they are safely buried.

An Irish youth proves his manhood by getting stuck in a pint, in a woman and in a fish — in that order.

The more you step on the dunghill, the more dirt you'll get in.

BITTERNESS

A cranky woman, an infant or a grievance should never be nursed.

A tongue of ivy — a heart of holly.

The begrudger is as important a part of Irish life as the muck he throws.

Many's the honest man was betrayed by a bitter stepmother.

It's the stones from their father's sloes that children choke upon.

More bitterness is caused by not making wills than by not making up.

A neighbour is comforting in failure and bitter in success.

Sneering does not become either the human face or the human soul.

BLESSINGS

A mother's love is a blessing.

It's a blessing to be in the Lord's hand as long as he doesn't close his fist.

Beware the blessing of a man crossed in love or at an auction.

A blessing is often an upside-down curse.

Don't bless with the tip of your tongue if there's bile at the butt.

May we always have a clean shirt, a clean conscience and a bob in the pocket.

May you be across Heaven's threshold before the old boy knows you're dead.

Here's to a wet night and a dry morning.

Thirst is a shameless disease so here's to a shameful cure.

That the tap may be open when it rusts.

Here's to absent friends and here's twice to absent enemies.

When you look at the world through the bottom of a glass may you see someone ready to buy.

Here's to the light heart and the heavy hand.

May the doctor's shadow never cross your right hand.

BORROWING

Borrowing borrows sorrowing.

Borrowed time brings no interest.

Never sleep with a strange woman or borrow from a neighbouring one.

The borrowed horse has hard hooves.

Better an old hat than a borrowed one.

You won't get rich borrowing from a begger.

The devil isn't the lender of borrowed time.

Borrow from a landlord, beg from a tenant.

Never borrow for what you don't need.
Never think you need what you have to borrow for.

BRAVERY

A brave man seldom loses.

He who faces disaster bravely can face his maker.

Every cock crows on his own dunghill.

There are more coats held in fights than there are blows struck.

If you're the only one that knows you're afraid, you're brave.

One brave man forms a majority.

Easier brave alone than in a crowd — except the crowd are brave too.

It is often braver to live than to die.

Bravery is always respected, even when concerned with ill-motive.

Being cowardly is being brave in retrospect.

Fortune favours the brave.

It's easy to stand your ground when only *skitogs* (strips of bogwood) are being flung.

The brave and the cowardly last the same length on the battle-field.

CHARACTER

You can take a man out of the bog but you cannot take the bog out of the man.

The mohair suit doesn't hide the bog-dirt under the fingernails.

Murder of the body makes a villian; murder of the character, a hero.

A fair character is a fair fortune.

A good man is not without fault and there are two faults in every man.

Better a man of character than a man of means.

Character is more precious than gold.

Even if you lose everything take care of your good name for if you lose that you are worthless.

You can't judge a man's respectability by the size of his prayer-book.

When you get lime on your *brógs* (boots) it's hard to shake it off.

What is in the dog comes out in the pup.

Empty vessels make most noise.

Don't measure a farmer by his acres but by his heart.

CHARITY

Constant begging meets constant refusal.

A charitable man has never gone to Hell.

The smaller the cottage, the wider the door.

Charity begins at home.

As you give, so will you receive.

Dispensing charity is the only advantage in amassing a fortune.

Give charity when you can. When you can't it will be too late to acquire the blessing of giving.

There's wool on the ditch that would make a coat for a poor man.

Neither charity nor virtue grows like the need for them.

CLEVERNESS

An té nach bfhuil láidir ní foláir dó a bheith glic. (The person that's not strong must be cute.)

That man cut his wisdom tooth on his mother's breast.

A Clare man would sleep in your ear and build a nest in the other.

Better to be clever than strong.

In spite of the fox's cunning, many a woman wears its skin.

The clever man discovers things about himself and says them about others.

He would mind mice at a cross-roads.

That fellow would cover a rock with hay and sell it as a haycock.

He's as cute as a church mouse and goes to the altar to learn, not to pray.

A clever crook dresses well.

She would drink the milk and say her cat was a thief.

COMMERCE

A verbal agreement is not worth the paper it's written on.

When the cards are on the table it's no time for playing the joker.

Hold on to the bone and the dog will follow you.

Better to have old debts than old grudges.

Short accounts make long friends.

If you buy what you don't want you might have to sell what you need.

Forgetting a debt doesn't pay it.

Better to go to bed supperless than to rise in debt.

People of the same trade are friendly — while they both keep their own customers.

The miller's pigs are fat but God knows whose meal they eat.

The lazy tailor has a long stitch.

He'll never meet a receiver for he'd give away nothing.

COMPANY

The man that's full of *nohawns* (sayings) will never have an empty hearth.

Show me your company and I'll tell you what you are.

If you lie down with dogs you'll rise with fleas.

Cherish company that does not carry woe on its sleeve.

Even the scabby sheep likes to have a comrade.

The loneliest man is the man who is lonely in a crowd.

When you want to be alone be sure there's no chink in the shutters.

I want his company as much as a *méagram* (headache) wants noise.

Avoid his company if he has eyes outside of his head like a good laying hen.

Constant company wears out its welcome.

People will meet but never the hills and mountains.

Company leaves with means.

Talk to yourself rather than to bad companions.

Make a dog your companion and you'll learn to bite.

If you want to be with the company you'll call it good company.

A fox won't keep company with a hound.

Don't keep company with your betters. You won't like them and they won't like you.

It's better to be alone than in bad company.

Better to be sick with company than lonely and alone.

COMPETENCE

Little is achieved without discipline.

The ebb-tide will not wait for the slow man.

If your messenger is slow go to meet him.

Every cripple finds his own way of dancing.

No use having a money-maker if you don't know how to work it.

Well lathered is half-shaven.

Well begun is half done.

When the hat is on the house is thatched.

Even if you are on the right track, you'll get run over if you just stay there.

The incompetent talk, the competent walk.

The man that knows what to overlook is the best trained in his job.

CONTENTMENT

Firelight will not let you read fine stories but it's warm and you won't see the dust on the floor.

Enough is as good as plenty.

A share is often enough.

What you haven't got you won't miss.

If you have one pair of good soles it's better than two pairs of good uppers.

If you want to be out of your house more often then you should be at home more often.

Be happy with what you have and you'll have plenty to be happy about.

The far-off hills are greener but the one you climb to work is not as steep.

27

A jug of punch, a warm woman's hand and I wouldn't call the Queen my aunt.

If you never come up in this world you'll never go down in the next.

The best days are when you cannot see him across the table with the pile of potato skins.

DEATH

There is no use in crying when the funeral is gone.

Ireland's only improving business is undertaking.

There are no pockets in the habit

Many a day we shall rest in the clay.

Death looks the old in the face and lurks behind youth.

May you never die until you see your own funeral.

Late to bed, late to rise,
Has a good man begging before he dies.

Nobody ever died of winter.

Death is the poor man's physician.

Funeral offerings will not buy salvation.

There's many a dry eye at a moneylender's funeral.

Never shave a corpse alone for fear your hand would slip and you'd be accused of murder.

There's no respect for the living if they ail during a long winter nor for the dead if their funeral is during harvesting.

The keening is best if the corpse left money.

Dead men tell no tales but there's many a thing learned in a wake-house.

No wise woman or herb can cure death.

A man at sea may come back but not a man in a graveyard.

Better the trouble that follows death than the trouble that follows shame.

The only thing worse than a mother's mourning is a mother's murderer.

There are more lies told in a wake-room than in a court-room.

Better an ounce of flour for the living than a ton of sympathy for the dead.

Though the marriage bed be rusty, the death bed is still cold.

You cannot tell whether the old sheep's skin or the young lamb's will hang from the rafters first.

DRINK

It's the first drop that destroys you; there's no harm at all in the last.

Daylight comes through the drunkard's roof the fastest.

A man takes a drink; the drink takes a drink; the drink takes the man.

There's no breaking the stranglehold of a Clonakilty Wrestler. (A local brew of the 1920s.)

You've never seen a flagday for a needy publican.

Before you call for one for the road be sure you know the road.

Practice makes perfect, there's many do think,
But a man's not too perfect when he's practised at drink.

Drink is the curse of the land. It makes you fight with your neighbour. It makes you shoot at your land-lord—and it makes you miss him.

Whiskey is the secret of longevity. When you take it to excess you have to work hard to lose the pounds and you have to work twice as hard to earn the pounds to pay for it.

A drink is shorter than a good yarn about it.

He'd step over ten naked women to get at a pint.

If Holy Water was porter he'd be at Mass every morning.

The devil invented Scotch whiskey to make the Irish poor.

The only cure for drinking is to drink more.

The longer the journey the shorter the time for knocking back the jar.

Don't shoot the fiddler. He owes the sheebeen too much.

A narrow neck keeps the bottle from being emptied in one swig.

A man in need of a drink thinks of wiser schemes than the great generals of our time.

There's little profit in constant drunkenness.

The truth comes out when the spirit goes in.

Morning is the time to pity the sober. The way they're feeling then is the best they're going to feel all day.

It's sweet to drink and sour to settle for it.

Thirst begets greater thirst.

He'll never comb a grey chair because of his drinking.

. . . some persons think more of a ball of malt than they do of th' blessed saints.   *O'Casey*

EDUCATION

A knowledgeable man frowns more often than a *duine le Dia* (person of God, a simple person).

What everybody know is hardly worth knowing.

No use having the book without the learning.

To address a head without knowledge is like the barking of a dog in a green valley.

It's no use trying to get an empty bag to stand.

You won't learn to swim on the kitchen floor.

A country's knowledge is contained in its language, mythology and mountains.

An educated man understands the half-word.

Youths and fools are hardest taught.

The pen is mightier than the sword—but only in the hand of a just man.

It's never too late to learn if you buckle down to it.

He met the scholars on the way home from school.

A knowledge of evil is better than evil without knowledge.

Learning is a light burden.

A backward child won't learn anything by starting at the end of the book.

If you keep giving your children comics they'll never read *War and Peace.*

A man that's fond of reading will never finish tidying his loft.

Don't start to educate a nation's children until its adults are learned.

A scholar's ink lasts longer than a martyr's blood.

The schoolhouse bell sounds bitter in youth and sweet in age.

Activity is the only road to knowledge.

Shaw

Education is an admirable thing, but it is well to remember from time to time that nothing that is worth knowing can be taught.

Wilde

ENEMIES

When an enemy offers you a favour, stay close to your own.

The best way to get rid of your enemies is God's way, by loving them.

Never meet an enemy in a fight or in court.

Better the coldness of a friend than the sweetness of an enemy.

A nation's greatest enemy is the small minds of its small people.

Bid good day to your enemy but listen for his footsteps behind you when you pass.

Put an Irishman on a spit and you'll soon have two Irishmen turning him.

Better fifty enemies outside the house than one inside it.

Little words and little enemies have to be closely watched.

EXPERIENCE

You can't teach an old dog new tricks.

The longer the pinkeen swims the less he sweats.

An experienced rider doesn't change his horse in midstream.

Never give a haikey (inexperienced youth) his will or a pup his fill.

An old broom knows the dirty corners best.

You won't catch an old bird with chaff.

The wearer knows best where the boot pinches.

You cannot know what's around the next bend of the road until you start walking.

Be a man's trade bad or good only by experience will he master it.

Experience is a hard school but a fool will learn in no other way.

The longest way 'round is the shortest way home.

If you know every weed in a boreen you'll not fall into its potholes.

An old dog sleeps near the fire but he'll not burn himself.

If a man fools me once, shame on him. If he fools me twice, shame on me.

Every dog is a pup till he hunts.

The lesson learned by a tragedy is a lesson never forgotten.

A burnt child dreads the fire.

It's no use opening the gate of opportunity if we have not learned to walk through it.

Experience is the name every one gives to their mistakes.

Wilde

FAMILY

You can't weigh worries but many a mother has a heavy heart.

Bricks and mortar make a house but the laughter of children makes a home.

Praise and scold in equal measure,
If your family you treasure.

Blood is thicker than water — and easier seen.

A wise boy makes his father happy but a foolish one is a mother's sorrow.

Children won't make you laugh at all times but neither will they make you cry.

Níl aon tinteán mar do thinteán féin. (There's no hearth like your own.)

What the child sees is what it does.

No man ever wore a scarf as warm as his daughter's arm around his neck.

The best wedding present you can give your child is the memory of a happy hearth.

An old man's child is hard to rear.

Your son is your son today but you have your daughter forever.

No matter how near your coat is to you, your flesh is nearer.

He is short of news that speaks ill of his mother.

Poets write about mothers, undertakers about fathers.

A family of Irish birth will argue and fight,
But let a shout come from without and see them all unite.

A mother with a purse is better than a father with a plough team.

There's trouble in every house and some in the street.

A family is never as close as when it's in mourning.

It's better to be haunted at home than hunted among strangers.

The family that has no skeleton in a cupboard has buried it instead.

No son is as good as his father in his sister's eyes. No father is as good as his son in his mother's eyes.

The herd gathers together when the wolf calls.

There's no love till there's a family.

Every mother thinks the sun rises on her own child.

A woman is never a mother till she has a son; a man is never a father till he has a daughter.

Children begin by loving their parents. After a time they judge them. Rarely, if ever, do they forgive them.

Wilde

FATE

If you're born to be hanged, you'll never be drowned.

Many a ship is lost near the harbour.

Nothing can be erased from God's book.

The apple will fall on the head that's under it.

No matter how long the day, night must fall.

The fox that leaves the covert when the hounds are in the glen seals his own fate.

A pitcher that's often taken to the well will get broken in the end.

Who's drowned in the storm is to be mourned — for after the storm comes the calm.

What brings death to one brings life to another.

Any man can lose his hat in a *side-gaoith* (fairy-wind).

If a man is his own ruin let him not blame fate.

An oak is often split by a wedge from its branch.

All good things must come to an end.

FIGHTING

Better to come in at the end of a feast than at the beginning of a fight.

Quarrelling dogs get dirty coats.

The quarrelsome man is lucky. Everybody has to put up with him except himself.

Keep in with the bad man for the good man won't harm you.

Better red wine than red blood.

Never get between a tree and its bark.

It's no use sticking a bayonet in a twister's gut unless you twist the bayonet.

Attackers can never be attacked.

If wars were fought with words Ireland would be ruling the world.

A shut fist won't catch a hawk.

When the leader falls, the fight stops.

If we fought temptation the way we fight each other we'd be a nation of saints again.

Better bear the palm than face the fist.

To attack is the best form of defence.

Have your ructions on your own battlefield.

The pup's mother teaches it to fight.

'Tis better to have fought and lost
Than never to have fought at all.

Fighting doesn't solve anything but it prevents it happening again.

A minute's parleying is better than a week's fighting

An Irishman is seldom at peace unless he is fighting.

He that fights and runs away will live to fight another day.

We fought every nation's battles and the only ones we did not win were our own.

Nothing is ever done in this world until men are prepared to kill one another if it is not done.

Shaw

The first blow is half the battle.

Goldsmith

As long as war is regarded as wicked it will always have its fascination. When it is looked upon as vulgar, it will cease to be popular.

Wilde

This contest is one of endurance and it is not they that can inflict the most, but they who can suffer the most who will conquer.

Terence MacSwiney

FLATTERY

Soft soap won't remove the dirt if it has been flung your way.

Soft words butter no turnips.

If you're going to tell a girl you're leaving her tell her she's beautiful first.

Imitation is the best form of flattery.

What really flatters a man is that you think him worth flattering.

Shaw

Yet each man kills the thing he loves,
By each let this be heard,
Some do it with a bitter look,
Some with a flattering word.

Wilde

FOOD

A fast cook causes a faster pain.

Kissing is as sweet as good cooking but it doesn't satisfy as long.

The crab tree has a sweet blossom.

There's a hard stone with the sloe.

It takes a lot of hard work to turn a bitter damson into a sweet jelly.

Food is gold in the morning, silver in the afternoon but lead at night.

A long churning makes bad butter.

There are more knobs in the buttermilk than what you see floating.

The first at the pot shouldn't be last at the work.

Butter's dear bought when it's licked off a briar.

Eat yourself into a doaghy dandilly and you'll dwine. (Eat yourself into an inactive, overindulgent youth and you'll ail slowly.)

When a stomach is full the bones like to stretch.

It's a good wife whose mouth is your mirror.

Any army may march on its stomach but a husband always makes love on it.

Feed him the finest brown bread and he'll stay,
But feed him on clokes and forever he'll stray.

A man at the food should be a man at the work.

You must crack the nuts before you can eat the kernel.

God give you better meat than a galloping hare.

He'd offer you an egg if you promised not to break the shell.

The first drop of soup is the hottest but the most wholesome lies below.

Eaten bread is soon forgotten — except when it's baked by a complaining wife.

Indigestion is gut jealousy.

The dog that buries his bones is either well fed or well advised.

The best eating is at the bottom of the stock-pot.

FOOLISHNESS

A fool and his money are easily parted.

There's a fool born every minute and every one of them lives.

It doesn't take much to make a fool laugh.

Only a fool burns his coal without warming himself.

There's no fool like an old fool.

Never take the thatch off your house to buy slates for a neighbour's.

Never call a Kerryman a fool till you're sure he's not a rogue.

Folly has a fall ahead of it.

It's as foolish to let a fool kiss you as it is to let a kiss fool you.

It's only a fool who won't get value from a borrowed horse.

FRIENDSHIP

A boy's best friend is his mother and there's no spancel stronger than her apron-string.

There's no war as bitter as a war between friends.

There's never an old *bróg* (boot) but there's the shape of a foot in it.

In times of trouble you know your friends.

There never was an old shoe without an old stocking to fit into it.

Two persons never lit a fire without disagreeing.

Friendship is love without its wars.

The best way to make friends is to meet often;
The best way to keep them is to meet seldom.

A friend's eye is the best mirror.

A little relationship is better than much friendship.

Prove your friend is not your enemy before you need a friend.

The only place you need a friend is in court or in battle.

A husband should use his wife's shoulder to cry on.

A friend in need is a friend indeed.

GOD

You worship God in your way and I'll worship him in His.

God gave us two ears and one mouth and we should use them in the same proportion.

God is good but don't dance in a *niavogue* (currach).

Nothing is impossible in the sight of God.

God is merciful but the Devil help us if He ever gets vexed.

God doesn't crave bickering, bitterness or bigotry — only love.

The nearer the church, the farther from God.

God's help is closer than the door.

Only the grace of God is between the saddle and the ground.

God helps them that help themselves.

Man proposes, God disposes.

The ways of God are strange.

If you haven't been taught by God you'll not be taught by man.

God is ill disposed to a lying tongue.

Only the Lord can save a racehorse from being a jackass.

Prayers from a black heart are like thunder from a black sky — neither are wanted by God nor man.

God is a powerful friend in times of distress.

God's help is always near.

GOODNESS

If better were within, better would emerge.

The heart of the roll is often the poorest.

Good begets good.

If you stretch out with your hand, you'll reach out with your feet.

The bag of apples is never full of rotten ones.

Goodness never comes late.

There's more good in a countryman's little finger than in the white hands of all the city's clerks.

The good that is is better than two goods that were.

Goodness is woman's greatest beauty.

GREED

The pages of books are too clean for some of the gallous deeds done for greed.

Every man is born clean, clever and greedy. Most of them stay greedy.

You can't take more out of a bag than what's in it.

The greedy pike gets caught the quickest.

The man who divided Ireland didn't leave himself last.

Gluttons have least taste.

The greedy man stores all but friendship.

Greed in a family is worse than need.

The greedy dog licks the honey on the briar.

HEALTH

Early to bed, early to rise,
Makes a man healthy, wealthy and wise.

It's often the poor man looks like he got a weekend ticket from Glasnevin.

A woman doesn't have to go out to get the best medicine for her man.

Every patient is a doctor after his cure.

A ship begins with a beam, a kiln with a stone, a king's reign with greetings but the beginning of health is sleep.

A swelled head won't hurt as much as a swelled toe but it's a far greater malady.

A good laugh and a long sleep are the best cures in the doctor's book.

Life's physician prescribes humour.

Eat an apple going to bed
Make the doctor beg his bread.

A long illness doesn't lie.

What cannot be cured has to be endured.

A curing stone is never too heavy a weight to carry.

Young blood should never be cold.

Obesity makes corpses hard to coffin and hard to carry.

Do not blame dampness for pains until you see a drink with rheumatism.

A healthy man is a king.

Begin with a cough and end with a coffin.

Work never killed a man but play is often the best medicine.

One must pay health its tithes.

The stout man thinks he gets enough exercise walking after thin men's funerals.

No time for your health today; no health for your time tomorrow.

If butter and poteen can't cure it, it's time to count it in the trimmings.

HEAVEN

If you have a roving eye it's no use having the other one fixed on Heaven.

The best matches are made in Heaven.

The best way to make sure you see a person in Heaven is to see little of him on earth.

There is not a tree in Heaven that's higher than the tree of patience.

Heaven's *leac na teine* (stone before the hearth) is reserved for the poor.

There are not enough Leinster men in Heaven to make a half-set.

The road to Heaven is well signposted but badly lit at night.

The shoulders under the coffin have often jostled the corpse out of Heaven.

HELL

The road to Hell is paved with good intentions.

The paving stones on the road to Hell have the weeds of lust binding them.

Needs must when the devil rides from Hell.

Card games were made in Hell.

The elbow on the bar counter points the way to Hell.

A drinking husband, a flighty wife,
Make Hell on earth of family's life.

Walk the road to Heaven but carry the map of Hell.

If you meet the devil leave room for him to pass.

Bid not the devil good day until you meet him.

What one gets over the devil's back will be spent under his belly.

HOPE

There's no flood that doesn't subside.

There are finer fish in the sea than have ever been caught.

It's a long road that has no turning.

A man in love keeps moping.
A woman in love keeps hoping.

Hope is the lazy man's spade.

God never sent hunger without something to satisfy it.

'I hope to' is a weak man's way of refusing.

He who has never hoped can never despair.

God never closes the door without opening another.

All is not lost that's in the floodmark.

The silver lining is often in the mind's eye.

Every cloud has a silver lining.

There's nothing that trouble hates facing as much as a smile.

There's nothing so bad that it could not be worse.

The bluebells are found in the deepest forest.

Even if love is not around the corner there's hardly a fight or you would have heard it.

There's no need to go to the Sceiligs if you smile till the next Shrove.

HUMOUR

If he has a purple countenance and no humour leave him to the priests.

It's a great thing to turn up laughing having been turned down crying.

A sense of humour is not a burden to carry yet it makes heavy loads lighter.

One man with humour will keep ten men working.

A man that can't laugh at himself should be given a mirror.

A woman in the home is a treasure; a woman with humour in the home is a blessing.

Humour, to a man, is like a feather pillow. It is filled with what is easy to get but gives great comfort.

The best humour comes from the kitchen.

When a thing is funny, search it for a hidden truth.

Shaw

HYPOCRISY

Even a tin knocker will shine on a dirty door.

Always check that there's bread under the butter.

The bigger the patch, the bigger the hole.

She who smiles at the door scowls in the kitchen.

The street angel is the house devil.

There is often a barb behind a kiss.

If there's honey on the tip of the tongue there's gravel in its butt.

She who kisses in public often kicks in private.

Before you shake the right hand of an enemy make sure he's not a *ciotog* (left-handed person).

A cat purrs before it scrapes.

The rose hides the briar.

You can't make a silk purse out of a sow's ear.

The man that hugs the altar-rails does not always hug his own wife.

He is no king who has no hostages under his ward in his Dún.

Brehon maxim

IDLENESS

A busy mother makes an idle daughter.

Poverty waits at the gate of idleness.

The devil finds work for idle hands.

Winter comes fast on the idle.

A foot at rest gets little spun.

Better to be knotting a *súgán* (hay rope) than to be idle.

You'll never plough a field by turning it over in your mind.

It's a worthless hen that won't provide for herself.

It's a poor family that can't afford one gentleman. It's a rich family that can't afford one idler.

Long sleep makes a bare backside.

Leisure is refined idleness.

Fireside talk is the talk of idle women.

INFORMERS

An informer can't mend his ways. He'll inform until he's in his grave and even then you should be careful with the first shovel full.

More Irish graves were opened by the mouth than by the shovel.

A whisper in an enemy's ear is louder than a shout from a mountain.

Keeping your tongue in your jaw is keeping healthy.

Easy on with the hay when the listeners are on the ladder.

INTEGRITY

A crooked cane makes a straight back.

Promise is in honour's debt.

What is got badly goes badly.

Real values have no jingle.

When rogues fall out honest men get what's theirs.

It's harder to become honest than it is to become rich.

You don't have to live with the man you cheat but you have to live with your conscience.

For man to be himself he must know himself.

Don't let worldly good divert you from protecting your pledge.

When an Irishman talks of 'principle' he is a danger to everybody.

O'Connor

The truth is rarely pure, and never simple.

Wilde

A little sincerity is a dangerous thing and a great deal of it is absolutely fatal.

Wilde

If one tells the truth, one is sure, sooner or later, to be found out.

Wilde

JUSTICE

God Almighty often pays his debts without money.

After the gathering comes the scattering.

If Ireland had acquired as much justice as abuse she would be the greatest nation on earth.

What's good for the goose is good for the gander.

Those who make the laws are often their greatest breakers.

There's no merriment in the seat of justice.

If he has the name of being a just man visit his home before you trust him.

To every cow its calf and to every book its copy.

King Diarmaid (c. 560)

For man's grim Justice goes its way,
And will not swerve aside.

Wilde

Do not do unto others as you would they should do unto you. Their tastes may not be the same.

Shaw

LOVE

Love is blind but the neighbours see through it.

A lad's best friend is his mother until he's the best friend of a lassie.

If she pleases the eye she'll please the heart.

Love is like stirabout, it must be made fresh every day.

Love at first sight often happens in the twilight.

If you live in my heart you live rent-free.

Old coals are easiest kindled.

After the settlement comes love.

If you love her in *giobals* (rags) your love will last.

There's little love until there is a fight.

Jarbles (rags) drop off quicker than tift (fine clothes).

Sheeps' eyes don't see beyond the settle.

Love is not an impartial judge.

Wiggy (light) turf burns bright but not for long.

If she has a mind of her own there won't be many with a mind for her.

Never cross a woman who has been crossed in love.

Wait till you're eighteen to marry and don't be spoiling your growth.

Love cools quickly.

A flicker that warms is better than a blaze that burns.

A broken love is a broken promise.

Weakening sight means weakening love.

If that fellow doesn't soon get a woman he'll he getting his thrills at the offerings.

Every thrush thinks her mate sings the sweetest.

What's nearest the heart is nearest the lips.

Once you break the ice it won't be long till you can lift the water.

Love is intoxicating. It pleases at first and then sends its victim reeling.

Love is like sun to a flower — it invigorates the strong but wilts the weak.

If a man is in love he is no judge of beauty but when love wears off he'll tell a woman about her warts.

There is no love sincerer than the love of food.

Shaw

LUCK

Better to be born lucky than rich.

Practice is everything and there's luck in leisure.

Lady Luck didn't flirt with many Irishmen.

The lucky shot won't kill the devil.

Good luck brings good wine with it.

The foolish have luck.

The daughter that's minding the parents is always in the byre when good luck is in the haggard.

The ugly are luckier than the handsome.

Good luck is better than early rising.

It's an ill wind that blows nobody good.

Never put the *mí-ádh* (bad luck) on your benefactor.

There is luck in sharing and pluck in refusing.

MAN

The man of the house needs three meals a day and four grouses.

Men are like bagpipes: no sound comes from them till they're full.

A man is a man when his woman is a woman.

A sea wind changes less often than the mind of a weak man.

Greatness in a man knows modesty.

A man's fame lasts longer than his life.

Every man to his own taste.

A man works hard for success and then squanders his time talking about it.

No man can prosper without his woman's leave.

Man can climb the highest summits, but he cannot dwell there long.

Shaw

A man who is not afraid of the sea will soon be drowned.

Synge

The reasonable man adapts himself to the world; the unreasonable one persists in trying to adapt the world to himself.

Shaw

MARRIAGE

Ride *cúlóg* (behind the rider) to the wedding, lead his horse to the christening.

Marry a scalder (unfledged bird) and she'll want to rove the world.

Marry in haste, repent at leisure.

A dumb wife and a blind husband might make their marriage work.

Marry a mountainy woman and you marry the mountain.

What harm if your man strays. He mightn't wish to be making a hack out of his best hunter.

A blanket is warmer when it's doubled.

Marriage changes a man and makes the woman that changed him whine about his not being the same man she married at all.

A shameful wife makes her husband stick out in a crowd.

Young people bother their parents about getting married. When they're married they are bothered themselves.

A bad wife takes advice from everybody except her husband.

The only thing in the world that's better than a good wife is no wife.

Let the man that you marry have an old maid for a mother.

No use buying a bandage for your wife's head when you've broken it.

What's all the world to a man when his wife is a widow?

A woman that marries too young or too old is the subject of gossip.

There'll be white blackbirds before an unwilling woman ties the knot.

Never advise an Irishman to marry or go to war — he's too hot-tempered for either.

The dowry drops over the cliff but the drooping lip remains on the wife.

He's walking her out that long 'tis an ease to the shoe-leather for them to be married.

It's a lonely washing that hasn't a man's shirt in it.

If you marry money the woman will outlast it.

He married a good woman but she didn't take off her boots yet.

Marriage and courting are the same except the settle is more comfortable than the haggard.

Marriages are all happy. It's having breakfast together that causes all the trouble.

Marriages may be made in heaven but the raw materials come from hell.

A boy gone wrong is a good man dead and a man married is a boy lost.

Most Irishmen have the same wife for life but she's not the same woman.

Marriage is popular because it combines the maximum of temptation with the maximum of opportunity.

Shaw

Whatever joys await the blest above,
No bliss below like happy wedded love.

Allingham

Women begin by resisting a man's advances and end by blocking his retreat.

Wilde

MEANNESS

He'd skin a flea for a ha'penny and sell the hide.

A mean act is long felt.

Small minds utter small words.

The mean deed turns on the man that did it.

She's so mean she'd get the cat to chew her meat in order to save her delph (false-teeth).

He wouldn't give you what would blind a *ciaróg's* (beetle's) eye.

If you lend your coat don't cut off the buttons.

He still has his confirmation money.

There's little difference between a closed hand and a fist.

If she's mean at the table she will be mean in the bed.

Meeting decency won't change the ways of a *bradaigh* (thieving cow).

They're so mean they'd give you one measel at a time.

He'd steal the cross off an ass's back.

He'd lift the cross off a cripple's beads.

MISFORTUNE

'Tis a misfortune for a man to cut a *bonnsog* (twig) to beat himself.

Beidh lá eile ag an baorach. (The underdog will have his day.)

You never miss the water till the well runs dry.

An Irishman sees his profit after his misfortune.

When misfortune is greatest, relief is nearest.

A man can shake hands with his misfortune without leaving his parish.

Only speak of misfortune when it comes calling.

It's easy to sleep on your neighbour's misfortune.

From strong relationships often comes great misfortune.

The latest misfortune is the greatest misfortune.

Misfortune sends no warning.

Butter on butter is a blue lookout.

MISTAKES

God only made one mistake — he allowed mistakes to happen.

When fools make mistakes they blame Providence.

You cannot mistake a man that owes you money or a woman that owes you love.

Take heed lest God mistakes your crawthumping for violence.

If you take the wrong hat from a meeting make sure it doesn't belong to a big man.

Do not mistake a *meigeall* (goat's beard) for a fine stallion's tail.

Correct your own mistakes from those made by others.

The wise man doesn't know his master's mistakes.

A man lives alone with his mistakes. A woman shares them.

MONEY

The best way to keep loyalty in a man's heart is to keep money in his purse.

Thirst after the drink and sorrow after the money.

The hardest man to tire is the money-lender.

Money borrowed is soon sorrowed.

Money is a good servant but a bad master.

Money taken, freedom forsaken.

Money is only money's worth.

A wage is the amount of money a man lives on; a salary is the amount he spends.

The unluckiest person to meet is not a red-haired woman but the man that lent you money.

Fame is dead if fame is bankrupt.

Money makes the mare go.

Inflation is when you have money to burn but can't afford a match.

A poor tinker would like to have a rich man's problems.

The man who asks what good is money has already paid for his plot.

A month before harvest the merchant sells nothing but money.

Money talks.

The man who pays the piper calls the tune.

Money is the root of all evil but avarice is the compost.

As the money bag swells, the heart contracts.

Wealth is an uncertain prop.

When I was young I thought that money was the most important thing in life; now that I am old I know that it is.

Wilde

NATURE

It costs nothing to see nature's great non-stop show.

Cast not a clout until May is out.

The brightest sunshine is after the rain.

A child that hasn't lived in the country enjoys only half a life.

Nature will come through the claws.

It only takes one bad potato to destroy what's on the *gais* (stalk).

The tallest flowers hide the strongest nettles.

A wildgoose never reared a tame gosling.

It takes every blade of grass to make the meadow green.

The cow doesn't always take after its breed.

Every bird as it's reared and the grouse for the bog.

What's in the marrow comes out in the bone.

There's no tree but has enough rotten twigs to burn it.

NEED

Words are as much needed as stones in Clare.

Necessity is a virtue.

If you are without sheep you have to be your own dog.

Need is the beginning of greed.

The man with a cow doesn't need a scythe.

He's so needy he couldn't give up eating his nails for Lent.

PATIENCE

A watched pot never boils.

Patience is a virtue,
Have it if you can;
It's seldom in a woman
And never in a man.

The slow horse reaches the mill.

The apple won't fall till its ripe.

Patience will heal the most itching scar.

Castles are built stone by stone.

If you push the carrier to the well he might fall in.

Night never yet failed to fall.

Patience is like love; you must have it to know about it.

Patience and forbearance made a bishop of His Reverence.

If you rush the woman the spuds will be hard.

Stepping stones will get you across the steam of life.

The cow won't have her calf till she's ready.

In a crowded bed it's better to wait to turn until father turns.

The greatest need for patience is when waiting your turn for the settle.

The hen with the egg is the least patient.

69

Patience cures many an old ill.

The only thing more blessed than patience is a silent woman.

Patience brings its own reward.

POLITICS

A week is a long time in politics.

A turkey never voted for an early Christmas.

A shrewd politician would see a flea copulating on top of Liberty Hall.

If you're going to abstain, do it in person.

A statesman is a dead politician.

The Dail is the only place in Ireland that is powered by hot air and where noise travels faster than light.

The last move in politics is reaching for the gun.

A politician is a man who can find a problem in every solution.

An ambassador is a politician who can do less harm away from home.

The successful political leader can divide the national cake so that everybody thinks he's getting a slice.

There's nothing like a few shots to change the fanatic into a non-partisan.

A patriotic politician will always lay down your life for his country.

He that England wants to win
Must with Ireland first begin.

When the pissmires get into government let them remember who fed them at haymaking time.

When the dirty work has been done at the cross-roads the main road is not so clean either.

Liberty means responsibility: that is why most politicians fear it.

In matters of grave importance, style, not sincerity is the vital thing.

Wilde

[A Political] Party is the madness of many for the gain of a few.

Swift

He knows nothing and he thinks he knows everything. That points clearly to a political career.

Shaw

PRIDE

Stoop as you walk the path of life and you'll not be struck by the branch of pride.

71

He fancies himself so much that his mother is trying to remember were the shepherds looking on when he was born.

Pride may have a fall and if it's family pride it brings a few with it.

You cannot soothe the proud.

Pride is the author of every sin

Pride never stops growing until it's ready to challenge God.

He's like a store bullock — proud but useless.

The gentry's pride prevents their seeing the beauty of humility.

PROPERTY

A good lease with a bad landlord is better than the best landlord in the country and no lease. Best of all would be the country without either landlord or lease.

The black drop is in the fairest graizer (larger farmer).

Half a loaf is better than no bread.

Possession is nine points of the law.

Have it yourself or do without.

Better to own a little than to want a lot.

A poor man never lost his property.

Your friends are as big as what you own
If that is small you're all alone.

If you don't own a mount don't hunt with the gentry.

Where there's a will there's a fray.

A dog owns nothing, yet is seldom dissatisfied.

Many an Irish property was increased by the lace of a daughter's petticoat.

Land and horses are properties dearest to an Irish heart.

Play with the woman that has looks, talk marriage with the woman that has property.

ROGUERY

Aithnigheann ciaróg ciaróg eile. (One rogue knows another. *Ciaróg* is a beetle.)

She'd cheat the devil in the dark and take two farthing candles for a ha'penny.

She's as crooked as a *creel* (basket) is watertight.

A rogue and a decent man shouldn't be mentioned in the same day.

He'd cod you out of the sight of your eye,
And tomorrow come back to steal off with the stye.

73

He was a rogue since he was knee high to a grasshopper.

You cannot plough a straight furrow in a crooked field.

Bribe the rogue and you needn't fear the honest man.

He'd wriggle his way out between the tree and the bark.

If he gives you a rope he might stand at your back while it's hanging you.

SCARCITY

Famine houses haven't as much in them as would baptise a fairy.

There's no bullock roaring inside a poor man's belly — if there is it's not roaring for turnips.

One shower in a drought is about as good as a grasshopper's spit.

Fruit is sweetest when it's scarcest.

You won't find many top landings in Ballymagorry.

Ireland's plenty is water in a *kesh* (basket).

You won't find many *pusthagauns* (conceited people) in the workhouse.

A crippled *ciarog* (beetle) could look over the heap of potato-skins on the table.

Snuff at a wake is fine if there's nobody sneezing over the snuff box.

There's little need to keep a cat when all the mice in the house will die of malnutrition.

SENSE

If commonsense rules from your head to your feet you'll not wear a dunce's cap or walk a wrong road.

Beware the woman that has more between her stays than between her ears.

Commonsense has its feet planted in the past.

On an unknown path it is better to be slow.

The man with sense doesn't talk before breakfast.

Sense bought by experience is better than two senses learned.

Don't put a giddy man at the tiller.

Even a rock of sense should move when there's danger.

The man who rows the boat does not rock it.

The gossips were all busy in the corner when God was giving out sense.

A little of anything is not worth a *thraithnín* (straw) but a little sense is worth a lot.

The sensible man finds now quicker than tomorrow.

It's no use sending a chicken to bring home a fox.

Never put a fox minding hens.

A blind man should not be sent to buy paint.

It's no use carrying an umbrella if your shoes are leaking.

If you don't fry over an open fire you'll never get burned.

Never promise a fish until its caught.

SORROW

There's nothing as sorrowful as a mother without her children.

Bid 'More power to your elbow' to the fiddler for joy, to the drinker for sorrow.

Happiness always has a little sorrow mixed through it.

Sorrow is supped from an arogant spoon.

A lone woman has a sorrowful row to hoe.

Be sorry for the jealous man.

There is often a tear behind a smile.

We learn in suffering what we teach in song.

SPENDING

Easy come, easy go
But having to spend what's hard got is a blow.

The son spends fast what his father hoarded long.

Spent money causes no rows.

If he doesn't spend when he's single, he won't give when he's not.

Don't give your purse to a lender
And don't give your heart to a spender.

If he gives a lodging he won't show you the road.

Money lent is money spent.

SPORT

You can't decide a tug-of-war contest by cutting the rope with a knife.

If I bet on the tide it wouldn't come in.

What you gain on the roundabouts you lose on the swings.

When the going gets tough the tough get going.

What you win on the field, you lose at the *saiseamh* (*Saiseamh* — wrestling at hurling matches of old).

If that goalkeeper put his head in his hands it would slip through.

It's no use feeding a forward with the ball if he hasn't been fed at the table.

Eternal hope means eternal hunger for the gambler's family.

Watching is part of good play.

The best hurlers are on the ditch.

STRENGTH

Muscles won't bend a strong man's will.

The strong obey when the stronger order.

The strong man may when he wishes; the weak man may when he can.

It's not the strongest that live the longest.

Where strength shows, strength grows.

The man with the strongest character is attacked most often.

TACT

Be nice to them on the way up. You might meet them all on the way down.

Don't crow till you're out of the wood.

A diplomat must always think twice before he says nothing.

Do not visit too often or too long.

Never talk about a rope in the house of a hanged man.

If you wish a favour from a man sit beside him.
If you wish a rebuke sit in his seat.

A tactful word is better than a pound in the hand.

Never talk about the blow that's not yet struck.

A cat doesn't sleep on a dog's sop.

Tact is clever humility.

If you say everything you want to say you'll hear something you don't want to hear.

TALK

A kind word never got a man into trouble.

Speak neither well nor ill of yourself.

Talk is cheap.

There's no bone in the tongue but it often struck a man down.

A slip of the tongue is no fault of the mind.

English is all-right for huckstering but the Irish language should always be used in lovemaking.

It's no use boiling your cabbage twice.

It's a bad thing not to have words on the tip of your tongue.

Soft words butter no turnips but they won't harden the heart of the cabbage either.

When the hand ceases to scatter the mouth ceases to praise.

It's not always what you say but who you pay that counts.

There's grit in the butt of a rival's praise.

No use wasting your words on a harm done.

Whisper into the glass when ill is spoken.

Kind words never split any man's lip.

Talking never got the hay saved.

He who comes to you with a secret to tell goes away with two.

You can easily win an argument if you start off by being right.

Leave the bad news where you found it.

There's no smoke without fire.

What's nearest to the heart is nearest to the mouth.

When a friend needs vocal support tongues get heavy.

Alehouse talk gets weaker with the night air.

Every man is wise till he speaks.

If words were nails we'd have built a great nation.

Empty heads keep open mouths.

Don't believe half of what you see or quarter of what you hear.

Silence is the fence around the haggard where wisdom is stacked.

Those who talk the loudest about a man while he is alive whisper the lowest in the mortuary.

Medicine goes in through the mouth but there's no medicine will save a fellow that uses his mouth too much.

Argument is the worst sort of conversation.

Swift

Questions are never indiscreet. Answers sometimes are.

Wilde

You need not praise the Irish language — simply speak it.

Pearse

THANKS

Say 'Please' to the judge for you won't be able to say 'Thanks' when the hangman's job is done.

Never look a gift horse in the mouth.

If you beg on a foolscap, don't thank on a postcard.

Give a dairymaid buttermilk but don't expect any thanks.

It's a good day when your thank-you bag is full.

THEATRE

A theatre critic doesn't serve his time to his trade — but he should serve time for his work.

An actor who says he doesn't read the reviews is neither a coward nor an egotist — he's a liar.

There are two types of theatre critic. One thinks he's God Almighty, the other is sure of it.

If there's coughing during the first scene they won't be using their hands for clapping.

Man is a creature of habit. You cannot write three plays and then stop.

Shaw

The world is a stage but the play is badly cast.

Wilde

TIME

Time and tide wait for no man.

Time is longest to the waiting man.

Time brings the sweetest memories.

Time will bring the snail to Jerusalem.

Time is the best *seanachaidhe* (storyteller).

Don't be too busy to kill time.

When God made time he made plenty of it.

Waste my money but don't waste my time.

The busy man is the man who makes time to help.

VALUE

The man that knows the price of everything knows the value of nothing.

83

True value comes in dull wrappings.

It's poor value a dog that's not worth the whistling.

An empty house gives better value than an owing tenant.

A shack is valuable to a poor man.

Give good value and the good will come back.

WEARINESS

It's as long as a wet Sunday and as dreary as a wet Easter.

A weary woman makes a weary bed.

Weariness often wears a smile.

If the knitter is weary the baby will have no new bonnet.

WISDOM

A man begins cutting his wisdom teeth the first time he bites off more than he can chew.

There's more wisdom spat into the *griosach* (embers) than you'd pick up in a year's booklearning.

Taking the second thoughts means taking the first steps to wisdom.

A questioning man is half way to being wise.

There's no wise man without some fault.

Fear of God is the beginning of wisdom.

The wisest words ever written were the ten commandments. The most foolish words were written by those who ignored them.

If you're ailing from over indulgence you'll not die of wisdom.

An apple can't grow on a crab tree and a wise man won't bear a fool.

The wise bird flies the lowest.

Wisdom makes a weak man strong, a poor man king, a good generation of a bad one and a foolish man reasonable.

The wisest man sees the least, says the least but prays the most.

A word to the wise is enough.

WOMAN

She mightn't be much good to boil a pot of spuds but she'd look lovely carrying them to the table.

Women would drive you mad but the asylum would be a cold place without them.

A dishonest woman cannot be kept in and an honest one won't.

There's nothing more vicious than a woman's temper except, maybe, a woman's tongue.

The foolish woman knows the foolish man's faults.

A jealous woman would make trouble between two breast bones.

There's nothing makes the windows (eyes) open like a fine doorful of a woman.

A whistling woman and a crowing hen,
Will bring bad luck to the house they're in.

I wouldn't like to be hanging by the neck since she was thirty.

The heat is often far back in the woman that's forward.

Only shyness or shame prevents a woman from refusing a man.

Man to the hill, woman to the shore,
Boy to the mill, youth to the whore.

It's as hard to see a woman crying as it is to see a barefooted duck.

It is not the most beautiful woman who has the most sense.

Everything dear is every woman's fancy.

Avoid the woman that has too many nicks in her horn.

A woman without is one who has neither child nor pipe.

Never be in a court or a castle without a woman to make your excuse.

The weak grip of a woman holds tighter than a vice.

A Tyrone woman will never buy a rabbit without a head for fear it's a cat.

A woman and a child are like a goat. If they're not in trouble, they're coming out of it.

An excuse is as near to a woman as her apron.

A woman's beauty never boiled a pot but her ugliness never filled either it or her.

It takes a woman to outwit the devil.

You'd want to be up early to catch a woman out and you'd want to be up late to catch her in.

An inch makes a world of difference when it's in a woman's nose.

Some women are like a Kilmallock fire — little warmth in them.

Wherever there are women there is talking and wherever there are geese there's cackling.

Where comes a cow, there follows a woman,
Where comes a woman, there follows trouble.

A bad woman drinks much of her own bad buttermilk.

Let her rant and rave as long as the sun is high and as
long as she's loving, close and tender when the sun sets.

Like Irish wolves, Irish women bark at their own
shadows.

A woman who looks at the window is edgy,
A woman who gazes into the fire is worried.

She's the heart of the roll,
If she gives you a roll;
Leave her back to the Zoo
If she won't give you two.

Dublin Rhyme

WORK

Bless the man that can take out half a bank of turf by
day and whitewash his *braicin* (shed) by night.

Science won't do anything that a hungry labourer and
two mules won't do.

A bit of hard work never harmed any man.

Work as if there was fire in your skin and you'll never
be without a fire in your hearth.

Work for one thing and you'll gain another.

Make hay while the sun shines.

It's better to like what you do than to do what you like.

Sow early, mow early.

The ass that brays the most eats the least.

A lazy man's best day is tomorrow.

The mason that lays fifty bricks will die no sooner than the one that lays twenty.

The willing horse is always loaded.

Well begun is half done.

Praise if you wish progress.

More colds were caught by damp fancy clothes than from the sweat of the brow.

Every mickle makes a muckle.

Constant dropping wears a stone.

Many hands make light work.

The best blows to strike for Ireland are the blow of the sledge on the anvil, of the axe on the block, of the flail on the stone.

If you'd prefer to be doing something else, you're working.

Hard work and good care take the head off bad luck.

It's harder to gather than to scatter.

It's not a delay to stop and sharpen the scythe.

You won't be able to tell how much money a man is earning by looking at his clothes but you will be looking at his wife's.

Work hard, work long and have nothing to worry about — but in doing so don't become the boss or you'll have everything to worry about.

Do your job well and eat your fruits with relish.

Results are not achieved by chance; they are worked for.

Those that do the talking at meetings never meet to work.

Work while the bit is in your belly,
Play when you're slack.

There is no need to fear the wind if your haystacks are tied down.

The lazy man says he will always be busy tomorrow.

Work is the refuge of people who have nothing better to do.

Wilde

* * * * *

Keep your nose in the copy, the pen in your hand and before you know it you'll have a book written.

* * * * *

MORE INTERESTING BOOKS

'BEFORE THE DEVIL KNOWS YOU'RE DEAD'
IRISH BLESSINGS, TOASTS AND CURSES

PADRAIC O'FARRELL

'May you be in heaven an hour before the devil knows you're dead.'

'May today be the first day of the best years of your life.'

'May the wind always be at your back.'

Hearing news of a death or marriage, consoling neighbours in sorrow or sharing their joy, looking for a husband or wife, saving turf or going fishing – Irish people had blessings and curses for every occasion. Luckily many of these sayings have survived. A few startling new ones have been added too!

SUPERSTITIONS OF THE IRISH COUNTRY PEOPLE

PADRAIC O'FARRELL

Irish country people believed that fairies were always present among them and that around the next corner or in the very next clump of thistles there might well be somebody lurking who would lead them to the crock of gold at the end of the rainbow. Fairies were good to mortals who observed the superstitions which called for leaving them food, not throwing out water without first shouting a warning on them, and so on.

DICTIONARY OF IRISH QUOTATIONS

SEAN SHEEHAN

Dictionary of Irish Quotations contains a highly enjoyable and varied selection of interesting, informative, intriguing, infuriating – and sometimes just witty – remarks made by Irish people on a number of topical subjects. The quotations included range from the fifth century to today and from the classical to the colloquial. There are over 150 authors from St Brigid to Sinéad O'Connor. Yeats and Swift are quoted here and Wilde and Joyce. So too are Maria Edgeworth and Mary Lavin; Robert Emmet and Roger Casement; Douglas Hyde and Mary Robinson; Sean Hughes and Neil Jordan ...

THINGS IRISH

ANTHONY BLUETT

Things Irish provides the reader with an entertaining and informative view of Ireland, seen through the practices, beliefs and everyday objects that seem to belong specifically to this country. Discarding the usual format of chapters on a variety of themes, the book uses short descriptive passages on anything from whiskey to standing stones, from May Day to hurling, in order to create a distinctive image of Irish life. The reader is free to roam from topic to topic, from passage to passage, discovering a wealth of new and surprising facts and having a number of misguided beliefs put right.

THE IRISH COOKBOOK

CARLA BLAKE

The Irish Cookbook fills a long felt need for a sound but attractive cookbook for people who would like to add to their culinary skills and try cooking Irish style.

Traditional Irish dishes are slightly adapted to suit present day tastes and methods and included are some modern Irish recipes using Guinness, Irish whiskey, Irish hams and Irish cheese.

All the basic methods for making soup and cooking fish, meat and vegetables are given with a selection of unusual recipes. Suggestions are also made about accompaniments to make a pleasantly balanced meal. There are recipes to see you through all occasions from family meals and 'Quick and Easy' snacks to dinner parties.

FAVOURITE IRISH STORIES

Selected by
ANTHONY BLUETT

The publication of *Favourite Irish Stories* coincided with the fiftieth anniversary of the Mercier Press, founded in 1944. The stories selected are among the best published by Mercier Press over the last half century.

The stories range from undoubted classics of Irish literature like the work of Padraic Pearse and Daniel Corkery, to more recent favourites like John B. Keane and Brian Cleeve. It also includes stories from the oral tradition, with a selection from Eric Cross' celebrated and controversial *The Tailor and Ansty* and stories from Eamon Kelly, Ireland's best-loved seanchaí.

IRELAND IN LOVE

Selected by ANTHONY BLUETT

Ireland in Love is a lively collection of some of the country's most striking and unusual love traditions.

Did you know, for instance, that purple orchids were used in 'coaxing' women in Kerry and white gander droppings were employed to secure the love of a man in Cork?

The book brings together a variety of original texts which offer advice, help or simply amusement on such questions as telling the future, casting charms, laying curses and of course, matchmaking. This collection also contains a selection of songs, sayings, quotations and poems, including an excerpt from the outrageous *Midnight Court*.

IN IRELAND LONG AGO

KEVIN DANAHER

Those who have only the most hazy idea of how our ancestors lived in Ireland will find enlightenment in these essays which range widely over the field of Irish folklife. Kevin Danaher describes life in Ireland before the 'brave new world' crept into the quiet countryside. Or perhaps 'describe' is not the right word. He rather invites the reader to call on the elderly people at their homes, to listen to their tales and gossip and taste their food and drink; to step outside and marvel at their pots and pans, ploughs and flails; to meet a water diviner; to join a faction fight; hurry to a wedding and bow down in remembrance of the dead.

In this book Kevin Danher has not only given us a well balanced picture of life in Ireland, but has also gone far to capture the magic of the written word.

FOLKTALES OF THE IRISH COUNTRYSIDE

KEVIN DANAHER

Nowadays there is a whole generation growing up who cannot remember a time when there was no television; and whose parents cannot remember a time when there was no radio and cinema. It is not, therefore, surprising that many of them wonder what people in country places found to do with their time in the winters of long ago.

People may blink in astonishment when reminded of the fact that the night was often too short for those past generations of country people, whose own entertainment with singing, music, dancing, cards, indoor games and storytelling spanned the evenings and into morning light.

Kevin Danaher remembers forty of the stories that enlivened those past days. Some are stories told by members of his own family; others he took down in his own countryside from the last traditional storytellers. Included are stories of giants, of ghosts, of queer happenings and of the great kings of Ireland.

A homely, heartwarming collection of tales from the Irish countryside.